The Snake in the Grass

Also by Kathleen Long Bostrom
From Westminster John Knox Press

Song of Creation

To the Beirkers,
with gratitude and affection

The Snake
in the *Grass*

The Story of Adam and Eve

Kathleen Long Bostrom

Kathleen Long Bostrom

Christmas 2003

Illustrated by Dennis McKinsey

Westminster John Knox Press
LOUISVILLE • LONDON

Book design by Teri Vinson
Cover design by Teri Vinson
Cover illustration by Dennis McKinsey

First edition
Published by Westminster John Knox Press
Louisville, Kentucky

This book is printed on acid-free paper that meets the American National Standards Institute Z39.48 standard. ⊗

PRINTED IN HONG KONG

03 04 05 06 07 08 09 10 11 12 — 10 9 8 7 6 5 4 3 2 1

Cataloging–in–Publication Data can be obtained from the Library of Congress.

ISBN 0-664-22592-6

To all the folks at Wildwood
Who told me that I could—and should—
Be playful with the written word
And with my sermons, preached and heard.
Now, turn the pages, take a look—
You'll find my sermon in this book!

I dedicate to you, my friends,
This book, with love that never ends.

Kathleen Long Bostrom
Wildwood Presbyterian Church

The sun was so warm
Shining down on the ground,
As we sat in the garden
And looked all around.
I said to my Adam,
"Just look at us two!

Already, we've run out
of fun things to do.
We've eaten our fill
And we've climbed all the trees;
For didn't God tell us
To do as we please?"

But, oh, we got bored.
We got bored.
     Bored!
          Bored!
               BORED!

Our lives were too calm,
Which could not be ignored.
And then something went *HISS!*
We could not miss that hiss!

We jumped
When we saw him come slithering past.
We jumped
At the sight of that Snake in the Grass.
And he said to us,

"Why do you look so downcast?
This garden is dull,
And your lives far from thrilling.
But we can have
Lots of good fun if you're willing."

"There are a few secrets
I think you should know."
He spoke in a voice
That was soothing and low.

Well, Adam and I—
We had nothing to say.
Our Father was out of the garden that day.

"You see that big tree?"
Said the Snake in the Grass.
"That marvelous tree?
Number One in its class?
That tree
With the fruit that is juicy and ripe?

Nobody will know
If you take just one bite."
I shook my head *NO!*
And I said to the snake,
"The fruit you suggest
Is the one we can't take."

"God told us, 'NO! NO!
You must listen to me;
You can eat every fruit
But the fruit of that tree.
That tree that you see
In the midst of the garden?

18

You eat from its fruit,
And you'll lose in the bargain.
You may *not* eat that fruit
You must leave it alone.
If you don't, then this garden
You'll have to disown.'"

But the snake said, "HA! HA!
You believe what God said?
If you eat of this fruit
You will both wind up dead?
Come on! You can trust me!
Would I tell a lie?

God knows if you eat,
It will open your eyes.
Then you'll be like God,
Knowing evil from good."
I said to the snake,
"Well, I guess that I could."

He said, "Take a bite.
Take a bite, my dear Madam.
And after you're done,
You can pass it to Adam."
I thought to myself,
"What do I have to lose?

God gave me the power
To pick and to choose."
So I took a big bite,
And then Adam did, too.
And that simple act,
Well, it changed our whole view.

We saw for ourselves
Once we ate of that fruit,
That all we had on
Were our own birthday suits.
And, oh, then
The shame!

All the shame!
  Shame!
    Shame!
      SHAME!

Of knowing
We had but our own selves to blame.

We gathered some leaves
And we covered our skin.
But we could not cover
The truth of our sin.
The truth of our sin
We felt deep down within.
The snake said so slyly,

"Now, isn't this odd?
I hear someone coming—
Oh, could it be *God?*
Now, no one has asked me,
But I do believe,
That God won't be happy
With Adam and Eve."

We heard God out walking
Among all the trees.
We both tried to hide
In the cool, evening breeze.

Then God said, "Where are you?
Oh, why would you hide?
Adam, where are you?
And where is your bride?"

"I'm here, God," said Adam.
"My wife is here, too.
We hid,
For we did not know what else to do.

But now since you asked me,
I guess I can tell.
We hid,
For you see, we're not dressed very well."

Then God said, "What is this?
Oh, what have you done?
Who told you that you should feel shame?
Who's the one?
Who ate of the fruit?

Of the fruit of that tree?"
We looked at each other and said,
  "HE!"
     "SHE!"
        ("we.")

"The snake made me do it!"
"The woman ate first!"
"The man did not stop me,
But that's not the worst!

The snake is the problem!
He twisted my arm!
Oh, what was he thinking
To bring us such harm?"

And then God said, "STOP!
I have heard quite enough!
I tried to protect you,
But you called my bluff.

You had it so easy.
You had all this stuff.
Now everything changes.
Your lives will get tough."

"Because you have done this,
And broken my trust,
Your dinner, O snake,
Shall be nothing but dust.

All people will struggle
With hard work and toil
Until you are joined
Once again with the soil."

God said this to us
In a very sad voice.
We both felt so bad
To have made such a choice.
We looked up at God,
And what else could we do?

We turned from the garden,
And left all we knew.
Oh, we were so foolish!
We both should have known!
But now we must learn
To make do on our own.

41

We'll never go back
To the way we once were.
The good life is over,
Of that I am sure.
We should not have followed

That bad snake's advice!
We should not have let ourselves
Lose paradise.
But lose it we did,
And at such a high price.

So, now you have heard
About Adam and Eve.
How God gave us Eden
But we had to leave.
Of how we allowed
That old snake to deceive.

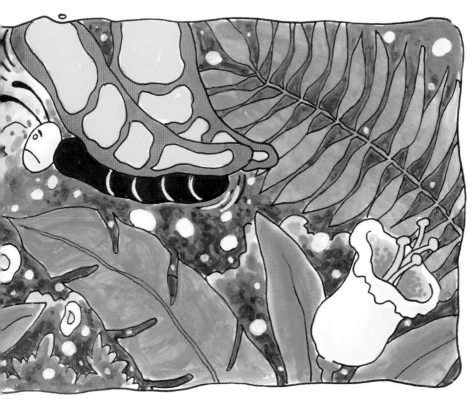

How neither of us
Would own up to our acts;
Though from the beginning,
We both knew the facts.
Have you ever said or done
Something that's wrong?
While knowing full well
It was wrong all along?

Then answer this question:
Just what will you say?
What will you say
When the Lord comes your way.

Do you always try
To be honest and true?
Tell me,
What will *you* do
When the Father asks you?